Anger

- Dada Bhagwan

Editor : Dr. Niruben Amin

Publisher : Mr. Ajit C. Patel
Dada Bhagwan Aradhana Trust
Dada Darshan, 5, Mamta Park Soc,
B/h. Navgujrat College, Usmanpura,
Ahmedabad-380014,
Gujarat, India.
Tel. : +91 79 3983 0100

First Edition : 3000 copies, January 2001
Reprint : 40000 copies, March 2003 to June 2016
New Reprint : 5000 copies, March 2017

Price : Ultimate Humility (leads to Universal oneness)
and Awareness of "I Don't Know Anything"

Rs. 20.00

Printer : Amba Offset
B-99, Electronics G.I.D.C.
K-6 Road, Sector-25,
Gandhinagar-382044, Gujarat, India.
Tel. : +91 79 39830341

<u>Trimantra</u>

The Three Mantras that Destroy All Obstacles in Life

Namo Vitaragaya
I bow to the One who is absolutely free from all attachment and
abhorrence

Namo Arihantanam
I bow to the living One who has annihilated all internal enemies
of anger, pride, deceit and greed

Namo Siddhanam
I bow to the Ones who have attained the state of total and final
liberation

Namo Aayariyanam
I bow to the Self-realized masters who impart knowledge of
liberation to others

Namo Uvazzayanam
I bow to those who have received the Knowledge of the Self and
are helping others attain the same

Namo Loye Savva Sahunam
I bow to all saints everywhere who have received the Knowledge of the Self

Eso Pancha Namukkaro
These five salutations

Savva Pavappanasano
Destroy all demerit karma

Mangalanam cha Savvesim
Of all that is auspicious

Padhamam Havai Mangalam
This is the highest

Om Namo Bhagavate Vasudevaya
I bow to all who have attained the absolute Self in human form

Om Namah Shivaya
I bow to all human beings who have become instruments for
salvation of the world

Jai Sat Chit Anand
Awareness of the Eternal is Bliss

Books of Akram Vignan of Dada Bhagwan

'Dadavani' Magazine is published Every month

Introduction to The 'Gnani Purush'

On a June evening in 1958 at around six o'clock, Ambalal Muljibhai Patel, a family man, a contractor by profession, was sitting on a bench on the busy platform number 3 of Surat's train station. Surat is a city in south Gujarat, a western state in India. What happened within the next forty-eight minutes was phenomenal. Spontaneous Self-realization occurred within Ambalal M. Patel. During this event his ego completely melted and from that moment onwards he became completely detached from all Ambalal's thoughts, speech and acts. He became the Lord's living instrument for the salvation of mankind, through the path of knowledge. He called this Lord, Dada Bhagwan. To everyone he met, he would say, "This Lord, Dada Bhagwan is fully manifest within me. He also resides within all living beings. The difference is that within me He is completely expressed and in you, he is yet to manifest."

Who are we? What is God? Who runs this world? What is karma? What is liberation? Etc. All the world's spiritual questions were answered during this event. Thus nature offered absolute vision to the world through the medium of Shree Ambalal Muljibhai Patel.

Ambalal was born in Tarsali, a suburb of the city of Baroda and raised in Bhadran, Gujarat. His wife's name was Hiraba. Although he was a contractor by profession, his life at home and his interaction with everyone around him was exemplary even prior to his Self-realization. After becoming Self-realized and attaining the state of a Gnani, (The Awakened One), his body became a 'public charitable trust.'

Throughout his whole life he lived by the principle that there should not be any commerce in religion, and in all commerce there must be religion. He also never took money from anyone for his own use. He used the profits from his business to take his devotees for pilgrimages to various parts of India.

His words became the foundation for the new, direct and step-less path to Self-realization called Akram Vignan. Through his divine original scientific experiment (The Gnan Vidhi), he imparted this knowledge to others within two hours. Thousands have received his grace through this process and thousands continue to do so even now. 'Akram' means without steps; an elevator path or a short cut, whereas 'Kram' means an orderly step-by-step spiritual path. Akram is now recognized as a direct shortcut to the bliss of the Self.

Who is Dada Bhagwan ?

When he explained to others who 'Dada Bhagwan' is, he would say:

"What you see here is not 'Dada Bhagwan.' What you see is 'A.M.Patel.' I am a Gnani Purush and He that is manifest within me, is 'Dada Bhagwan'. He is the Lord within. He is within you and everyone else. He has not yet manifest within you, whereas within me he is fully manifest. I myself am not a Bhagwan. I too bow down to Dada Bhagwan within me."

Current link for attaining the knowledge of Self-Realization (Atmagnan)

"I am personally going to impart siddhis (special spiritual powers) to a few people. After I leave, will there not be a need for them? People of future generations will need this path, won't they?"

~ Dadashri

Param Pujya Dadashri used to go from town to town and country-to-country to give satsang and impart the knowledge of the Self as well as knowledge of harmonious worldly interaction to all who came to see him. In his final days in late 1987, he graced Dr. Niruben Amin with the siddhis to continue his Work.

After Param Pujya Dadashri left his mortal body on January 2, 1988, Dr. Niruben continued his Work, traveling within India to cities and villages; and going abroad visiting all continents of the world. She was Dadashri's representative of Akram Vignan, until March 19, 2006, when she left her mortal body entrusting all further care of the Work to Shri Deepakbhai Desai. She was instrumental in expanding the key role of Akram Vignan as the simple and direct path to Self-realization for modern times. Hundreds of thousands of spiritual seekers had taken advantage of this opportunity and are established in the experience of pure Soul while carrying out their worldly duties. They experience freedom, here and now while living their daily life.

Shri Deepakbhai Desai had been given the siddhi to conduct satsang of Akram Vignan by Gnani Purush Dadashri in presence of Pujya Niruben Amin. Between 1988 and 2006, he has given satsang nationally and internationally as directed by Dadashri under the guidance of Dr. Niruben Amin. Now these satsangs and Gnan Vidhis of Akram Vignan continue in full force through the medium of Atmagnani Shri Deepakbhai Desai.

Powerful words in scriptures help the seeker in increasing their desire for liberation and thus they represent the path. The knowledge of the Self is the final goal of all seekers. Without the knowledge of the Self there is no liberation. This knowledge does not exist in books. It exists in the heart of a Gnani. Hence, the knowledge of the Self can only be acquired by meeting a Gnani. Through the scientific approach of the Akram Vignan, even today one can attain Atmagnan, by meeting a living Atmagnani. Only a lit candle can light another candle!

Note About This Translation

Gnani Purush Ambalal M. Patel, popularly known as Dadashri or Dada or Dadaji, used to say that it is not possible to exactly translate his satsang on the Science of Self-Realization and the art of worldly interaction, into English. Some of the depth and intent of meaning to be conveyed to the seeker, would be lost. He stressed the importance of learning Gujarati to precisely understand all his teachings.

Dadashri did however grant his blessings to convey his original words to the world through translations in English and other languages. It was his deepest desire and fervor that the suffering human beings of the world attain the living freedom of the wonderful Akram Vignan that expressed within him. He further stated that a day would come when the world would be in awe of the phenomenal powers of this science.

This is an humble attempt to present to the world the essence of the teachings of Dadashri, the Gnani Purush. A lot of care has been taken to preserve the tone and message of his words. This is not a literal translation of his words. Many individuals have worked diligently for this product and we remain deeply thankful to them all.

This is an elementary introduction to the vast new treasure of his teachings. Please note that any errors committed in the translation are entirely those of the translators and for those we request your pardon.

PREFACE

Anger is a weakness, but people think of it as strength. The one who does not get angry possesses more inner strength than the one who gets angry.

A person usually becomes angry when things do not go his way, when he is misunderstood by another person, or when his viewpoints clash with another's viewpoints. We become angry when we are accused of being wrong, when we think we are right. Our perception causes us to believe that we are right. According to the other person, he believes that he is right. Because we do not know how to reason and because, we have no foresight or intuition, we become angry.

When we are insulted, we become angry. We become angry when we incur a loss. In protecting our pride or our greed, we experience anger. If one is to become free from pride and greed, he must have awareness (spiritual). Say for instance, your son-in-law broke your china tea set, would you not control your temper? If your servant were to do the same thing, should you not control your temper in this situation as well? Our reactions vary in different situations (from situation to situation).

Anger can only dissolve if one understands that those who do wrong by him are merely his nimits, (people instrumental in delivering the effects of his past karma) and that what he is experiencing is the result of his karmas from his previous life.

We should be aware of our anger at all times. When someone is hurt by our anger, we should be remorseful, ask him or her for forgiveness, and vow never to get angry again. It is necessary for us to do this. We must do this because the person we become angry towards will be hurt; he will harbor a grudge and bind vengeance against us, and therefore, in our next life, we will have to suffer the consequences.

When parents become angry with their children or when a guru becomes angry with his disciples, they bind punya (merit karma). This is because their aim is to improve their children and disciples respectively. If one were to become angry out of selfishness, he would then bind paap (bad karma). This is the teaching of the Enlightened Ones.

Anger, the subject dealt with in this book, is the most troublesome and overt of all inner human weaknesses. It is discussed extensively for clear understanding. It is our sincere hope that the readers will find this helpful in their endeavor to free themselves from the severe grip of anger.

- Dr. Niruben Amin

ANGER

WHO ACCEPTS THEY ARE WRONG?

Questioner : If someone makes us out to be wrong even though we think we are right, we become angry with him. How can we stop from getting angry?

Dadashri : Yes, but only when you are right. Are you really right? Do you know that you are right?

Questioner : Our soul tells us we are right.

Dadashri : In that situation, you are the judge, the lawyer, and the culprit. So of course you are going to be right, you will not allow yourself to be wrong. Just as you think that *you* are right, the other person will think that *he* is right. Do you understand?

THESE ARE ALL WEAKNESSES

Questioner : Is it not good to feel an aversion towards injustice? Are we not justified in feeling angry when we clearly see injustice ?

Dadashri : Anger and hatred are weaknesses. The whole world has these weaknesses. Do you get angry if someone scolds you ?

Questioner : Yes, I do.

Dadashri : So is that a weakness or strength?

Questioner : In certain situations it is necessary to become angry.

Dadashri : No, no. Anger is a weakness. To say that anger is necessary in certain situations is a worldly notion. People make such statements because they are not able to get rid of their anger.

A PERSON IS STRONG WHEN HE REMAINS UNAFFECTED

Questioner : Would it not be considered cowardly to remain silent when someone insults you?

Dadashri : Not at all, to bear an insult is a sign of great strength. If someone were to swear at me right now, I would not have a single negative thought towards him. That is strength. Quibbling and quarrelling is weakness. To bear an insult calmly is a great strength. If a person overcomes an insult just once, he will acquire the strength to do so hundred times over. Do you understand? If you are strong, your opponent will become weak. That is the natural trend. When a weak person harasses us and we do not do anything in response, it is considered a great strength.

In actuality the weak should be protected and the strong should be confronted. In this current time cycle, nobody behaves in this manner at all. Nowadays, people keep badgering the weak and run away from the strong. There are very few people that protect the weak and stand up against the strong. This whole world keeps hurting the weak. At home, the husband dominates the wife. If you beat a cow that is tied up, where will she go? And what if you were to untie the cow and then beat her? She would either run away or fight back.

A man who, despite being strong, does not harm his opponents, not even his enemy, is considered a powerful person. Is it not cowardly when you get angry with someone who gets angry with you? I am saying that these inner enemies of man, anger, pride, attachment, and greed are weaknesses. Why would a person who is strong need to get angry? People, however, try to control others with their anger. Those who do not use anger as a weapon have something else. That something else, is *sheel* (extraordinary moral character). Sheel in a person subdues even animals. Lions, tigers, and enemies will all surrender to such a person.

THE ANGRY MAN IS A WEAKLING

Questioner : But Dada, what should we do when someone gets angry with us?

Dadashri : They will get angry. Is it under their control? Their inner machinery is not under their control. This machinery keeps working any way it can. If it were under their control they would not let the machine overheat. To become even the slightest bit angry is to behave like a beast. One becomes transformed from a human being into a beast. People would not let such a thing happen, but what can they do when it is out of the their control?

The world is such, that there is no reason at any given time for any anger to take place. Even when children do not listen, there is no reason to become angry. You must handle this situation by remaining calm. To become angry is a terrible weakness. Anger is the worst weakness of all. You should be sympathetic towards the person who becomes angry and understand that he does not have any control in this matter. You should feel compassion for the person who has no control over himself.

What does it mean to become angry? When one becomes angry, it is like setting fire to oneself and then setting others on fire. Once the match is struck, it bursts into flames, destroying all around. So if getting angry were under one's control, one would not get angry. Who likes to burn? If someone tells me that anger is necessary in this world, I would respond by telling him that there is never a reason for anger. Anger is a weakness and that is why it happens spontaneously. God has called it a weakness. God has said that a real man is the one who has no weakness of ego, anger, greed, or attachment whatsoever. These men that you see around you are weaklings, because they have no control over their anger and they do not know how to deal with it. Anger, ego, attachment, and greed are all obvious weaknesses. Can you not feel your body tremble when you get angry?

Questioner : Even the body is saying that anger is not good.

Dadashri : Yes, even the body tells us that it is wrong when it trembles. So, one should consider anger to be a great weakness.

PERSONALITY WITHOUT WEAKNESS OF ANGER

Questioner : If we see a man beating a child, should we not voice our anger at him?

Dadashri : He will not stop the beating even if you *do* get angry. Why would you get angry with him? He may beat you too. Talk to him calmly and explain to him that it is a weakness to react in anger.

Questioner : Then should we let him continue to beat the child ?

Dadashri : No, but you should ask him why he is beating the child. Try to make him understand. If you get angry with him, then this anger is your weakness. First and foremost, you should not carry the weakness within you. Those that do not have any weaknesses, have impressive personalities. When such people utter even a single word, everyone will listen to them readily.

Questioner : Perhaps they may not.

Dadashri : They would not listen to you because you

are weak and lack personality. There should not be any weakness. One should have good conduct. One must have a flawless personality. Even thugs will run away at the sight of such a person. No one will run away from an angry person. On the contrary they may even beat him up. The whole world strikes at the weak.

When can one acquire such a personality? He will acquire such a personality when he understands the spiritual science of the Self. In this world, the relative knowledge is forgotten, whereas the science of the Self remains with you.

FROST IS MORE DEADLY THAN HEAT

Dadashri : When there is frost or an ice storm, it gets so cold that it burns the grass, the trees, and all the crops. Why do you think everything burns when it gets cold?

Questioner : Everything burns because of extreme cold.

Dadashri : Yes, so if you live calmly and remain cool, you will become more effective.

DIGNITY WHERE ANGER CEASES

Questioner : But Dada, is it not a weakness to be too calm?

Dadashri : We have to remain within limits. That is called normality. "Below normal is the fever, above normal is the fever, and ninety-eight degrees is the normal". Therefore only normality is required.

People are more fearful of those who do not get angry as opposed to those who do. Why is that so? It is because one develops inner strength when anger ceases. This is the law of nature. Otherwise, there would be no one to protect such people. People use anger as a form of protection. In ignorance (ignorance of one's real Self), one's protection is through anger.

IRRITABLE PEOPLE ALWAYS LOSE

Questioner : Reasonable annoyance or reasonable anger, is it not good?

Dadashri : What do people call that? Even children will say, "He is always cranky!" It is foolish to become irritated. Irritation is considered a weakness. If we ask the children what their father is like, they would say that he is a very cranky person. Does this not discredit the father's reputation?

If you ask a child who in his family he likes best, he would say that he likes his mother the most because she does not get angry. The father undoubtedly comes last on his list because the father always gets angry. I would remind the child that it is his father who provides everything for him, so is not the father his favorite? And the child would shake his head. Now tell me, we work hard, we feed them, we bring home the money and give it to them, and yet even then we come last.

ANGER IS BLINDNESS

Questioner : What is the main reason behind a man's anger ?

Dadashri : He loses sight. When one does not see the wall, he bumps into it. In the same way, he cannot see from within, which is why anger occurs. When he cannot see what lies ahead of him, anger overcomes him.

ANGER OCCURS WHERE THERE IS LACK OF INSIGHT

When does anger take place? It is when one's vision (*darshan*) becomes obscured, and his knowledge (*gnan*) is obstructed, that his anger arises. The same happens when a person is overcome with pride.

Questioner : Please illustrate this point with an example.

Dadashri : Do people not ask you why you get angry?

You would tell them that it was because you could not think clearly. Yes it is when people cannot think clearly that they get angry. Would they get angry if they were able to think? How are you rewarded when you get angry? First the sparks set you on fire and then you burn others.

THE FIRE OF ANGER BURNS ONESELF AND THEN OTHERS

Anger is like putting a lighted match to one's own home. Anger is setting fire to one's own home, which is filled with hay. First his own house burns and then the neighbor's house.

What happens when a single match is thrown onto a haystack in a field?

Questioner : It will burn.

Dadashri : It is the same with anger. Whatever he had earned in two years, he will destroy in an instant by getting angry. Anger is a live fire. The person himself will not realize that he has destroyed everything, because the damage is not visible on the outside, but everything from within is destroyed. Part of whatever he has accumulated for the next life is expended. What happens if more is exhausted? As a human, he eats bread, but in his next life, as an animal, he will have to eat grass.

No man in this world can conquer anger. Anger has two parts. One part comes as discord and the other as restlessness. Discord is apparent to others and restlessness remains within, unseen by others. It is the discord part of anger that one is able to overcome. However, as one part is suppressed, the other part increases. When one claims to have conquered his anger, his pride increases. In reality, anger cannot be completely conquered. Perhaps one can say that he has conquered the visible anger, discord.

SULKING IS ANGER

When a person sulks in anger, it is really anger itself. For example, if a husband and wife quarrel intensely in the night, so much anger is generated that they both lay awake restless, the entire night. In the morning the wife serves him tea by banging the teacup. The husband will then realize that she is still sulking. This is called anger. The sulking can last for any period of time. For some it may even be life-long. Sometimes anger between a father and son will create such enmity between them that neither of them will want to see each other's face. The sulking is apparent from the disgruntled look on one's face.

Sulking can be such that, if someone were to insult me fifteen years ago, and I encounter him again today, the moment I lay eyes on him, I will remember everything from the past. That is *taanton* (the lingering connection from the past event). Ordinarily people's sulking never goes away. Even renowned ascetics and monks sulk. If you were to provoke them and challenge their authority, they would not speak to you for weeks. This is called taanton.

DIFFERENCE BETWEEN *KRODH* (ANGER) AND *GUSSO* (ANNOYANCE)

Questioner : Dada what is the difference between annoyance and anger?

Dadashri : Anger is associated with ego. When annoyance and ego are combined, they result in anger. When a father gets annoyed with his children, it is not called anger, because it is not associated with the ego. Anger binds *paap* (bad karma), but the annoyance of a father will bind *punyas* (positive karma), because he is thinking about the welfare of his children. Anger is accompanied by the ego. When you get annoyed, do you feel bad from within?

There are two kinds of anger, pride, attachment and greed (*krodh, maan, maya, lobh*).

One kind you can divert – *nivarya.* If you get angry with

someone then from within you divert that anger and calm it down. If one were able to reach this stage, his worldly interactions would become very pleasant.

The other kind of anger is one that cannot be diverted *anivarya*. One tries very hard to prevent it, but from within the explosion still occurs. Such anger is anivarya. This anger injures the person himself, as well as others.

God has allowed a certain level of anger for the *sadhus* (sages, monks) so that they may uphold the austerity of their conduct, as long as it does not hurt anyone. 'My anger can hurt only me and not anyone else.' This much anger has been permitted.

RECOGNIZE THE KNOWER

Questioner : We all know that anger is bad, but still…

Dadashri : It is like this : The one, who is angry, is not aware of the anger. The one, who is greedy, is not aware of his greed and the one who is arrogant is not aware of his pride. The 'knower' is completely separate from all of these weaknesses. People inquire why weaknesses still occur even when they are aware of their weakness. Now, who is it that says 'I know'? They do not know the answer to this. They are not aware of who the 'knower' is. This is what one must discover. If one can unearth the 'knower,' then all of his weaknesses will dissipate. It can only be called true knowledge, when all the weaknesses are destroyed.

KNOW THE CORRECT SOLUTION JUST ONCE

Questioner : I still become angry even though I know that it is wrong to become angry. What is the solution?

Dadashri : Who is it that knows? If you had the real knowledge just once, there would be no anger. But because you still become angry, it means that you do not know. There is ego in your saying that you know.

Questioner : After getting angry I realize that I should not get angry.

Dadashri : No, but after you know who the knower is, there would be no anger. Let's say there are two identical bottles standing side by side, and you are told that one has medicine in it and the other has poison in it. Now if you mistake one for the other, then you can conclude that you did not know. If you do not mistake the one for the other, then you can say that you do know. This would apply to anger as well. The reason you become angry is because you do not know. You are merely going around with ego when you say that you know. In darkness you are likely to bump into things, but when there is light and you can see clearly, you will not have any accidents. When we confuse the darkness with light, it is our own mistake. So come and sit in the Satsang with me and acquire the real knowledge. Then only will anger, pride, attachment, and greed go away.

Questioner : But everyone gets angry.

Dadashri : Ask this gentleman. He is saying no.

Questioner : There will be no anger after coming to satsang.

Dadashri : What kind of medicine do you think he took? It is a medicine that removes the root cause of anger.

ONLY THROUGH RIGHT UNDERSTANDING

Questioner : I get angry with people that are close to me. The other person may be right according to his viewpoint, but from my viewpoint I become very angry. What is the reason for my anger?

Dadashri : If you are walking along and a stone from a building falls on your head and hurts you, will you get angry?

Questioner : No, because it happened spontaneously.

Dadashri : No, but why do you not get angry in this situation? It is because you do not see anybody there. Who will you get angry with?

Questioner : But no one has thrown the stone.

Dadashri : And if you were to go out now and a little boy throws a stone at you, you will get angry with him. Why? Because you believe that the boy threw the stone at you. However, if a stone rolls down a hillside and hits you, you will look around but you will not get angry.

You become angry because in your mind you feel that a person is responsible. No one is able to hurt another person knowingly. Whether a boy throws a stone at you or whether a stone accidentally falls on you, it is essentially the same thing. It is an illusion that makes you perceive that someone is responsible for it. In this world, no man has the independent power over even his own bowel movements.

We *do* have control over anger. When we realize that no one has thrown the stone that falls from the hillside, we do not get angry. And when you say, "Anger overcomes me," it really does not. If it did, then why do you not react in the same way when a stone fall on you? Why don't you get angry when a policeman tells you off, yet you get angry with your wife, with the children, with the neighbors, and with those working under you? Why don't you get angry with your boss? Anger does not just happen to people. People get angry because they want to have their own way.

Questioner : How can one control it?

Dadashri : The control is present. Recognize that the person who throws the stone at you is merely your nimit (someone instrumental) who is bringing to you, the effects of your past karma. When you see a stone falling from a hill, your anger does not arise. In the same manner, here too you should exercise control, because everything is just like the hill.

If a car is coming head-on at you, will you get angry or will you move out of the way? Would you crash with the car? You are aware of the consequences. But when you get angry, the internal destruction is much greater. The external destruction is obvious to you, but you are not aware of the internal destruction. This is the only difference.

RESULTS CHANGE WHEN CAUSES CHANGE

Someone asked me why, for countless lives, man has tried to get rid of anger and has not succeeded. I told him that perhaps he did not have the right solution. He told me that the solutions given in the scriptures, which he himself was following, did not eradicate his anger. I told him that the solution has to be exact and correct. Trying to find a solution to stop the anger is foolishness because anger is a result. It is just like the results of an examination. The result cannot be changed. It is the cause which one needs to change.

People try to suppress anger, but it is futile, and in doing so one may even become insane. Besides, anger is not something that one can rid himself of. A person told me that he has been successful in suppressing his anger to some degree. However, you cannot say that it is suppressed, while it still remains inside. When he asked me for a solution, I told him to make note of those circumstances and those people that made him angry and to make note of those that did not. He also was to make note of when he did not get angry even though the other person did something wrong. There are circumstances in which we get angry even though the other person does the right thing. What is the reason behind this?

Questioner : Is it because a *granthi* (a knot of opinion) has formed in our mind for that person?

Dadashri : Yes, numerous opinions have been formed.

What should one do to disentangle from those opinions? The examination has already been given. You will get angry with that person as many times as you were meant to. But what must you do from now on? You should not allow yourself to become prejudiced towards the person with whom you get angry. You should change your opinion of him. It is because of the account of your *prarabdh* (fate, past karma, destiny) that this person is behaving in such a manner with you. Whatever that person does, it is because of the result of your own karma. You should change your opinion about him. If you change your opinion of him, you will no longer get angry with him. The effect from the past will remain for some time. That effect will come, give its results and then it will cease altogether.

This is a very subtle point, which people have failed to discover. There is a solution for everything. All matters in this world can never be without a solution. People are trying to destroy only the results. The solution to anger, pride, attachment, and greed, is to destroy their causes and leave the results alone. If one does not have the awareness in the first place, then how will he find the solution?

Questioner : Please explain again how to destroy the causes.

Dadashri : If I get angry with this gentleman, I decide that my anger towards him is the result of me seeing faults in him previously. Now whatever wrong he does, as long as I do not let it affect my mind, the anger towards him will subside. Some of it will still come as a result of the past, but no more will come in the future.

Questioner : Does anger stem from looking at others' faults?

Dadashri : Yes. Even while seeing their faults, you should be aware that it is wrong and it is a result. Once this process of seeing faults in others ceases, anger will cease.

EGO IS AT THE ROOTS OF ANGER

Some people ask how they can get rid of their anger. When they tell me that they try to suppress it, I ask them whether they are trying to suppress it *before* or *after* they understand it. I tell them that they must understand anger first, because anger and peace coexist. If one fails to understand anger and tries to suppress it, he may be suppressing peace instead, so peace will die. Therefore, anger is not something that one can suppress. One has to understand that anger is ego. Analyze the ego that causes the anger.

If this child breaks something valuable and we get angry, what kind of ego is it? It is the kind of ego that tells us that we have incurred a loss from the breakage. Here the ego is of profit and loss. We have to think about how we will go about destroying this kind of ego. Otherwise by harboring the ego, the anger will continue. Anger and greed at their very core, are really only ego.

WITH WHAT UNDERSTANDING IS ONE TO PACIFY ANGER?

Anger itself is the ego. One must examine why this is so. Once we look into it, we will be able to grasp it. If we get angry when something breaks, we have to question why the anger occurs. The answer would be that the breakage means a loss. It is because of the loss that we feel angry. If one thinks deeply about the ego and the anger, the very process of thinking will wash away his ego. There are circumstances that are unavoidable. The head of the household will scold his servant for breaking things, but he would remain silent if his son-in-law were to do the same. He remains silent with the people he considers important and he yells at the servant, whom he considers to be inferior. This is egoism. Do people not become silent in the presence of their superiors? If Dada were to break something, not even a single thought would cross their minds, but if the servant were to break something, then what? Even if people understood with their *buddhi* (intellect), it would suffice! If the buddhi had been developed and molded with understanding, then there would be no arguments. Will the scolding help restore the damage? It only gives one a little satisfaction. Moreover, there is bickering and mental stress involved in it.

In the above situation, one has not only incurred a loss from the broken cups, but also a loss from inner restless has been created. Thirdly, a loss has occurred because of hostility created towards the servant. The servant thinks that he is being cruelly treated because he is poor. He will harbor hostility and will bind revenge karma for next life. God has said that one should not bind vengeance with anyone. Where possible, bind love but do not bind hostility. If you bind love, then that love itself will destroy the hostility. Love overcomes hatred. Vengeance will breed vengeance and it will continue to do so forever. Vengeance is the reason for the endless wanderings life after life. Why do these human beings wander endlessly?

What obstacles arise? Where do the obstructions arise? We should destroy them. It is because of one's shortsightedness that he encounters obstructions. The Gnani Purush gives you the 'long-sight' that will enable you to see things exactly the way they are.

WHEN ONE GETS ANGRY WITH CHILDREN...

Questioner : What should I do when I become angry with my child ?

Dadashri : Anger happens because of lack of understanding. If you ask your child how he feels when you get angry, he will tell you that it hurts him. He is hurt and you are too. Is there a need to get angry with the child? If it benefited him, then you could continue with it, but if the consequences are bad, then what is the point of being angry ?

Questioner : If we didn't get angry then they wouldn't listen to us, and they wouldn't eat.

Dadashri : So you would intimidate them so that they would listen to you?

JUST LOOK AT THE SUBTLETY OF THE ENLIGHTENED ONES

People will think that a father is worthless because he displays so much anger towards his child. But what sort of justice would this be according to nature? According to nature's law, the father is binding punya. Why is it considered a punya in spite of his anger? It is because he is subjecting himself to turmoil for the benefit of his child. He binds punya because he takes on the strife for the happiness of his child. Generally all forms of anger will bind paap, except where one becomes angry and sacrifices his own happiness for the happiness of his child or his disciple. Here, punya is bound. People will look upon him with disgust and disapproval. The justice of nature is different. There is no *hinsak bhaav* (intention to hurt) when you become angry with your sons or your daughters, but there is hinsak bhaav everywhere else. His *taanto* (lingering of annoyance and anger) however, may remain and if so, whenever he sets eyes on his child, the conflicts will arise inside him.

Now if neither the intent to hurt nor the lingering of annoyance were present in the anger, one would attain liberation. If just the hinsak bhaav is missing, but the taanto is still there, then one would bind punya. Just look at the intricate details of discovery of The Lord.

DESPITE ANGER ONE BINDS PUNYA

God tells us that any anger that is done for the sake of others and for the benefit of a greater good, will bind punya.

Now in the Kramic path (the traditional step by step path to Self-Realization), religious disciples live under the fear of being reprimanded by their guru. The guru's eyes become red with anger. Yet, because he becomes angry for the welfare of his disciples, the guru binds punya. Can you imagine how much suffering they have to endure? How is one ever going to be liberated? Liberation is not easy. Only on a rare occasion does one attain something like AkramVignan.

ANGER IS A KIND OF A SIGNAL

People would say that the man that gets angry with his children is the offender and that he is the one that binds paap, but God does not say that. God would say that he is the offender if as a father he fails to get angry with his child. Is it good to get angry? No, but it was necessary at the time because if he did not, his son would have strayed in the wrong direction. Consequently, anger is a red signal, nothing else. If the father had not appeared intimidating and had not become angry, he would have lost his son to the path of vice.

People have no idea that anger is a red flag. It is important for one to understand when and for how long this flag has to be utilized.

FROM NEGATIVE TO POSITIVE MEDITATION

If you become angry with your son, your *bhaav* (intention) should be, 'This should not happen.' This means that you have changed negative meditation into positive meditation. Although you were angry, the result turns positive internally because you have changed your true inner intent.

Questioner : Is it because of the bhaav : 'It should not be this way?'

Dadashri : There is no intent to hurt behind it. It is impossible to have anger without the intent to hurt. Amongst all the different situations where anger occurs, it only binds punya when it is directed towards one's children, one's friends, and one's wife, if the intent to hurt is absent. The reason is clearly visible when one looks at his aim behind his anger.

Even anger has been divided. It is a different anger when you get angry with your son when he is not paying attention to the business. God has said that when a father gets angry with his son for stealing money and other misdeeds, the father will bind punya.

THE WAY MUSLIMS DEAL WITH ANGER

Questioner : We take out our anger on the wife when we cannot get angry with the secretary or the nurses at the hospital. She gets the worst part of it.

Dadashri : I tell people in satsang that when some men are reprimanded by their superiors, they vent their anger on their wives instead. So then I rebuke them and ask them why they are taking it out on their poor wives. I ask them why they do not fight with the person that scolds them instead of fighting with their wives.

A Muslim friend of mine invited me to his home, so one day I went with him. He only had two rooms in his house. I asked him how he managed to live in such a confined space. I asked him if his wife ever bothered him. He said that sometimes his wife would get angry but he would not. If they both were to get angry at each other, how would they be able to sleep in the same room? And furthermore, he would not get even a decent cup of tea in the morning. He told me that he was happy to be with his wife, so how could he get angry with her. And when she got angry with him, he would pacify her by sweet-talking her. He said that he would fight outside the home, but never in the home.

But our men (Hindus) on the other hand, would come home after receiving a mental thrashing outside and pass it on their wives.

All day long they are angry. Even the cows and buffaloes are better; at least they do not get angry. Life should be peaceful! There should be no weakness in our lives. Anger takes place all too often.

Did you come here by car? What would happen if the car got angry on the way here?

Questioner : Then it would be impossible to come here.

Dadashri : When you get angry with your wife, how do you think she copes?

Dadashri : (To the wife) You don't get angry do you?

Questioner : Sometimes it happens.

Dadashri : What's the use of you both getting angry?

Questioner : Should there not be some anger between a man and wife?

Dadashri : No. There is no such rule. There should be harmony between a husband and wife. If they hurt each other they are not husband and wife. There is never any heartache where there is true friendship, and this is considered the greatest of all friendships. Others have brainwashed you into thinking that this is the rule because it happens to them as well. There should not be any hurt between a husband and wife. It may happen in other relationships.

PUNISHMENT FOR OBSTINACY

Questioner : When we have conflicting opinions with our friends or with our family or when things do not go our way, we get angry. Why do we become angry? And what should we do about it?

Dadashri : Why do you even think about having your own way? What would happen if everyone did as they pleased? Instead you should think what would happen if everyone around you were stubborn and unyielding. You should never try to make things go your way. If you do not have any expectations, you will not go wrong. Anyone with expectations can be stubborn if he wants to. This is how you should look at it.

Questioner : No matter how hard we try to remain silent, what should we do when the men get angry?

Dadashri : If you want to start a quarrel, then you should also get angry. And if not, then you should just remain silent.

What use is anger to you? The person himself does not get angry. Anger is the effect of a "mechanical adjustment," which is why he later regrets it and wishes it never happened.

Questioner : What should I do to calm him?

Dadashri : When a machine gets too hot, you must leave it alone for a while and in a short time it will cool down. But if you keep meddling with it, you will get burnt.

Questioner : My husband and I get into terrible arguments and we also say hurtful things to each other. What should I do?

Dadashri : Is he the one who gets angry or is it you?

Questioner : Sometimes I do.

Dadashri : Then you should scold yourself from within. Ask yourself why you are getting angry when you know that you will suffer the consequences. Do *pratikraman* (the act of asking for forgiveness), and all your faults will come to an end. Otherwise you will have to suffer the same pain that you are inflicting. You will calm things down a little with pratikraman.

THIS IS CRUDE BEHAVIOR

Questioner : When we get angry we start using abusive language. How can we improve ourselves?

Dadashri : This happens because one does not have any control. In order to have some control one should first understand how he feels when someone gets angry with him. How does he tolerate such behavior when it is directed towards him? Treat others the way you would like to be treated.

If someone uses abusive language towards you and it does not bother you or depress you, it is a different matter. You should stop it altogether. One must never use abusive language. Swearing is crude behavior, unbecoming of any human being.

PRATIKRAMAN : THE REAL PATH TO LIBERATION

At one time people were taught to have compassion, practice fairness and forgiveness, but nowadays how can they have these qualities when they keep getting angry?

I would tell these people that whenever they get angry, they should repent from within. They should know the weakness within them, which prompts their anger. They should accept their mistake and feel remorse. If they have a guru, they should seek help from him. They should make a firm resolve to never let their weakness overcome them again. They should not defend their anger and they should do pratikraman for it. They should make a note of when, where, and with whom they became angry during the day and they should do pratikraman for it.

What should one do in pratikraman? If one's anger hurts another person, he must recall the Soul within that person and ask to be forgiven. He should ask forgiveness for his actions and vow never to do it again. *Aalochana* is confession of your mistake. When you confess your mistakes to me, you are doing aalochana.

ASK FOR FORGIVENESS INTERNALLY

Questioner : Dada, sometimes when we do pratikraman and repent for a mistake for getting angry with someone, we feel anguish within. Yet, we do not have the courage to ask for forgiveness face to face, from the person.

Dadashri : You need not ask for forgiveness in that way, otherwise the other person might misuse it. He may think that he has put you in your place. Just ask for forgiveness internally, by recalling the Soul within that person. There are only a handful of people who would forgive you before you even ask for their forgiveness. Such nobility is rare these days.

SINCERE PRATIKRAMAN YIELDS IMMEDIATE RESULTS

Questioner : Sometimes I become so angry that I will say something and then keep quiet, but I am in turmoil from within and this lingers on. Does this call for more than one pratikraman?

Dadashri : If you do pratikraman two or three times wholeheartedly and with resolve never to repeat the mistake, then everything is over with. Pray to the Soul within that person and confess that you became very angry and hurt him and that you are now asking for forgiveness for your actions.

FAULTS END ULTIMATELY

Questioner : The excitement stirred up through *atikraman* (aggression involving anger, pride, attachment, greed) is calmed down with pratikraman.

Dadashri : Yes, it does indeed calm down. With 'sticky files' (Dadashri's term for those with whom you have great attachment or abhorrence due to past life karma) you have to do more than five thousand pratikramans or so before things are squared away. Although you may not vent your anger when you become frustrated, if you do not do pratikraman, the 'stain' will not be erased. With pratikraman, everything is cleared up. If you do atikraman, then you must do pratikraman.

Questioner : What if you get angry with someone and you immediately ask for forgiveness on the spot ?

Dadashri : After acquiring Gnan, when you get angry, there is no problem, as long as you ask for forgiveness, because doing pratikraman will set you free. And if you cannot directly ask for forgiveness from that person, you should do it internally and this will also set you free.

Questioner : You mean in front of everyone?

Dadashri : It is fine if you cannot directly ask for forgiveness and you do it internally. These faults are lifeless and in the form of 'discharge' (Dadashri's term for the dissipation of effects of previous causes. The term 'discharge' applies only for those who have been graced with his separation from cause and effects of karma, in the Gnan Vidhi). A 'discharge' fault means that it is non-living, which means that the consequences will be minimal.

THE SENSE OF DOERSHIP SUSTAINS ANGER

You are not the one making things happen. It is the *kashayas,* the weaknesses within you of anger, pride, attachment, and greed that run everything. Only the rule of these kashayas prevails. When you acquire the knowledge of your real Self, these kashayas leave. When one gets angry, he feels remorse but of what use is it if he does not know how to do pratikraman? One is freed when he knows how to do pratikraman.

How long can these kashayas last? The kashayas will remain as long as one believes; 'I am Chandulal.' This belief gives support to the sense that the kashayas are his, 'I am angry, I am unhappy etc.'

It is when one attains the awareness, 'I am pure Self' that the sense of 'I am Chandulal' is broken and the kashayas are destroyed. Without this awareness all efforts to remove kashayas, in fact perpetuate them. When one's anger is controlled through his ego, the ego increases and when greed is overcome with the ego, the ego increases.

WHERE THE ANGER IS CONTROLLED, THE PRIDE INCREASES.

A sadhu told me that he had completely eradicated his anger through his spiritual effort. The anger was in fact suppressed. I told him that he had instead created a monster by the name of pride (*maan*). This monster thrives because he is the offspring of ignorance of the Self (*maya*). The sons of ignorance cannot be killed. One can get rid of them if he has a solution. This solution is Self-realization.

ANGER AND DECEIT ARE FALSE PROTECTORS

Anger and deceit give protection to pride and greed. The protector of greed is deceit and the protector of pride is anger. Sometimes deceit also plays a role in protecting pride. Sometimes anger also plays a role in protecting greed.

Through anger they practice greed. A greedy person rarely gets angry, and when he does, we should understand that he is probably experiencing some difficulty related to his greed. Moreover, greedy people do not care what others say or think as long as they make money. They do not care even if they are insulted. They are like this because deceit will protect them. Deceit is their ignorance and is part of their nature. Thus deceit and anger are protectors of internal weaknesses.

One gets angry when his pride is wounded. Anger is easily detected and therefore, is easy to remove as compared to deceit, which deceives even the owner. Anger is the first of the kashayas to go. Anger is like ammunition, and wherever there is ammunition, there is an army ready to fight. Once the ammunition is depleted, why would the army still fight? Everyone would simply run away. No one will stick around.

THE NATURE OF ANGER

Anger represents volatile atoms. If a barrel containing

gunpowder ignites, it would start an explosion. When all the gunpowder is finished, the barrel becomes inactive again. That is how it is with anger. The volatile atoms of anger will ignite according to the law of *vyavasthit* (Scientific circumstantial evidence), and will explode in every direction. It is not called anger (krodh) if no *taanto* (link of anger) remains. It is called anger only when there is taanto associated with it. It is called anger when there is a feeling of burning inside. When this happens, the burning continues and it affects others also. This burning if manifested outwardly, is called *kadhapo*, and if one experiences internal burning and restlessness, it is called *ajampo*. Sulking occurs in both.

TO ENDURE OR RETAIN A GRUDGE IS ANGER

If people do not use angry words, then it does not hurt anyone. It is not just the anger that is expressed outwardly that constitutes anger, but also the smoldering one feels within. Tolerance is really twice the anger. Tolerance means to suppress continually. One will realize this when the spring of coil suppressed anger rebounds one day. Why should one have to endure this? One merely has to bring about a solution through Gnan.

ANGER IS VIOLENCE

The intellect makes one emotional and Gnan keeps him calm. What would happen if a train running smoothly becomes emotional?

Questioner : An accident would occur.

Dadashri : If it does not stay upright on the track, there will be an accident. Similarly, when a man becomes emotional, so many living organisms within him are killed. The moment anger arises, millions of lives are destroyed, but even then people maintain that they practice non-violence (*ahinsa or ahimsa*). People need to be aware that they are doing great violence when they become emotional and get angry.

THE WAY TO CONQUER ANGER

The external activities of the world : the thoughts, speech, and acts of human beings do not change. However, if one changes his *bhaav* (deep inner intention), then it is enough.

People say they want to stop their anger. One cannot stop it immediately. Firstly, he must recognize what anger is and the causes behind it are. How is it born and who are its parents? All this has to be determined even before anger is understood.

LIBERATION AT THE HANDS OF THE LIBERATED

Do you want to be rid of your weaknesses? Tell me what you want to get rid of. Make a list. Are you bound by anger, pride, attachment, and greed?

Questioner : Yes.

Dadashri : How can a person who is bound, free himself? How can someone whose arms and legs are tied up tightly become free?

Questioner : He has to get help from someone.

Dadashri : Should he seek the help of someone who himself is tied up?

Questioner : He should get help from someone who is free to help.

Dadashri : Yes, you have to ask help from a person who is free.

THE FOOD OF ANGER, PRIDE, ATTACHMENT AND GREED

There are many people who have some awareness and insight into their anger. They say that they do not like the anger that develops within them. Many on the other hand believe that unless they get angry, they will not accomplish anything.

Anger, attachment, pride and greed always harm the owner. People do not understand this. If you were to starve them for three years, they (kashayas) would run away. What is the nourishment for these weaknesses? How can you starve them if you do not know what they thrive on? It is your lack of understanding that provides sustenance for them. How do they survive and carry on life after life? Stop feeding them. People do not think along these lines and instead forcefully try to subdue them. These four weaknesses will not go away easily.

An *acharya* (spiritual head) scolds his disciple with anger. If a person asks the acharya why he is scolding his disciple, and he replies that the disciple needed to be told off, then by making such a statement, he has fed his anger. This support for his anger is its food.

If anger, pride, attachment, and greed are not fed for three years, they will leave. This is because each has its specific diet, which people provide everyday and so they grow healthy and strong.

When a man smacks his child in anger, his wife will rebuke him for doing so. If he tells her that the child deserved it, then he would be feeding his anger. In making such statements, people support their weaknesses.

I have never given protection to anger, pride, attachment, and greed. If I happen to get angry and someone asks me why, I would tell him that it is wrong to get angry and that it occurred because of my weakness. In this way, I do not protect it. But other people do.

If a *sadhu* (an ascetic) happens to be using snuff and we ask why a man of his status should have such an addiction, he will strengthen his addiction when he says that there is no harm in using snuff.

Out of these four, anger, pride, attachment and greed, a person may favor one over the others and will therefore strengthen it by siding with it.

OVERT KARMA : SUBTLE KARMA

I will explain to you what overt (*sthool*) karma is. Do you ever become angry even though you do not want to be angry?

Questioner : Yes.

Dadashri : You experience the consequences of your anger right away. People will say that you are foul tempered. Someone may even slap you, which means that you will suffer the consequences through being disgraced in some way or another. Anger is *sthool* karma. When you get angry, if you have the internal bhaav that anger is necessary, then this bhaav will be your account of anger for your next life. If however, your bhaav today is that you should not get angry and you have made a decision that you do not want any part of anger, even though it still occurs, you will not have bound anger for the next life. You will be punished for the anger, which occurs as sthool karma in this life, but even then it will not bind you in the next life. This is because in the subtle (*sookshma*) karma your resolve (*nischaya*) is not to get angry.

On the other hand, if a person does not get angry with anyone, but has the belief that one should use anger to sort people out, then in his next life he will be a very angry man. Therefore, the external anger represents sthool karma and the internal bhaav is the sookshma karma. Sthool karma do not bind new karma. They represent an effect. That is why I have presented this science to you in a different light. Until now, people have been led to believe that karmas are bound through sthool karma, and that is why they live in fear.

KASHAYAS FLEE WITH THE SCIENCE OF SEPARATION

Questioner : Is there any prerequisite needed to conquer these four kashayas?

Dadashri : When these four kashayas of anger, pride, attachment, and greed leave, one becomes a God.

God said that when one gets angry with his blood relatives, their minds become estranged. This estranged state will prevail for years, or throughout their lives. Such anger is wrong. Ultimately it is a useless anger. This type of anger binds one for infinite lives. Even greed, pride, and attachment will do the same. They are very difficult. It is only after they leave, that one attains bliss.

One will be rid of these kashayas, if he listens to the Enlightened One. The Enlightened One is the Gnani Purush, who has the knowledge of the Soul and can give you this knowledge.

The only other way out from these kashayas is to acquire the Science of Separation. Then all these kashayas will leave. This is the wonder of this time cycle. This is called Akram Vignan.

- Jai Sat Chit Anand

Persons to Contact

Dada Bhagwan Parivar

Adalaj : **Trimandir**, Simandhar City, Ahmedabad-Kalol Highway, Adalaj, Dist.: Gandhinagar - 382421, Gujarat, India. **Tel :** (079) 39830100, **Email :** info@dadabhagwan.org

Rajkot : **Trimandir**, Ahmedabad-Rajkot Highway, Nr. Targhadiya Cross Road, Maliyasan Village, Rajkot. **Cell.:** 9274111393

Bhuj : **Trimandir**, Behind Hill Garden, Airport Road, Near Sahyognagar, Bhuj (Kutch). **Tel. :** (02832) 290123

Anjar : **Trimandir**, Anjar-Mundra Rd, Nr. Sinogra Patiya, Sinogra Village, Ta - Anjar. **Tel. :** 9924346622

Godhra : **Trimandir**, Village-Bhamaiya, Opp. FCI Godown, Godhra, Dist.-Panchmahal. **Tel. :** (02672) 262300

Morbi : **Trimandir**, Village-Jepur, Morbi-Navlakhi Road, Morbi, Dist.-Rajkot. **Tel. :** (02822) 297097

Surendranagar : **Trimandir**, Nr. Lok Vidyalaya, Surendranagar-Rajkot Highway, Muli Road, Surendranagar. **Tel. :** 9737048322

Amreli : **Trimandir**, Liliya road bypass chokadi, Kharawadi, Dist - Amreli. **Tel. :** 9924344460

Vadodara : **Trimandir**, Nr. Babaria College, Vadodara-Surat Highway, NH-8, Varnama Village. **Tel. :** 9574001557

Ahmedabad : **Dada Darshan**, 5, Mamtapark Society, B/h. Navgujarat College, Usmanpura, Ahmedabad- 14. **Tel. :** (079) 27540408

Vadodara : **Dada Mandir**, 17, Mama ni Pol (Street), Opp. Raopura Police Station, Salatvada, Vadodara. **Cell. :** 9924343335

Mumbai : Dada Bhagwan Parivar, **Cell. :** 9323528901

Bangalore : Dada Bhagwan Parivar, **Cell. :** 9590979099

U.S.A. : **DBVI Tel. :** +1 877-505-DADA (3232), **Email :** info@us.dadabhagwan.org

U.K. : **Dada Darshan (UK)** Tel. :+44 330-111-DADA (3232), Email : info@uk.dadabhagwan.org

Kenya : +254 722 722 063   **Singapore** : +65 81129229
Australia : +61 421127947   **New Zealand:** +64 21 0376434
UAE : +971 557316937   **Germany** : +49 700 32327474

www.dadabhagwan.org, www.dadashri.org